D1215181

The FIRST BOOK of

HOW TO RUN A MEETING

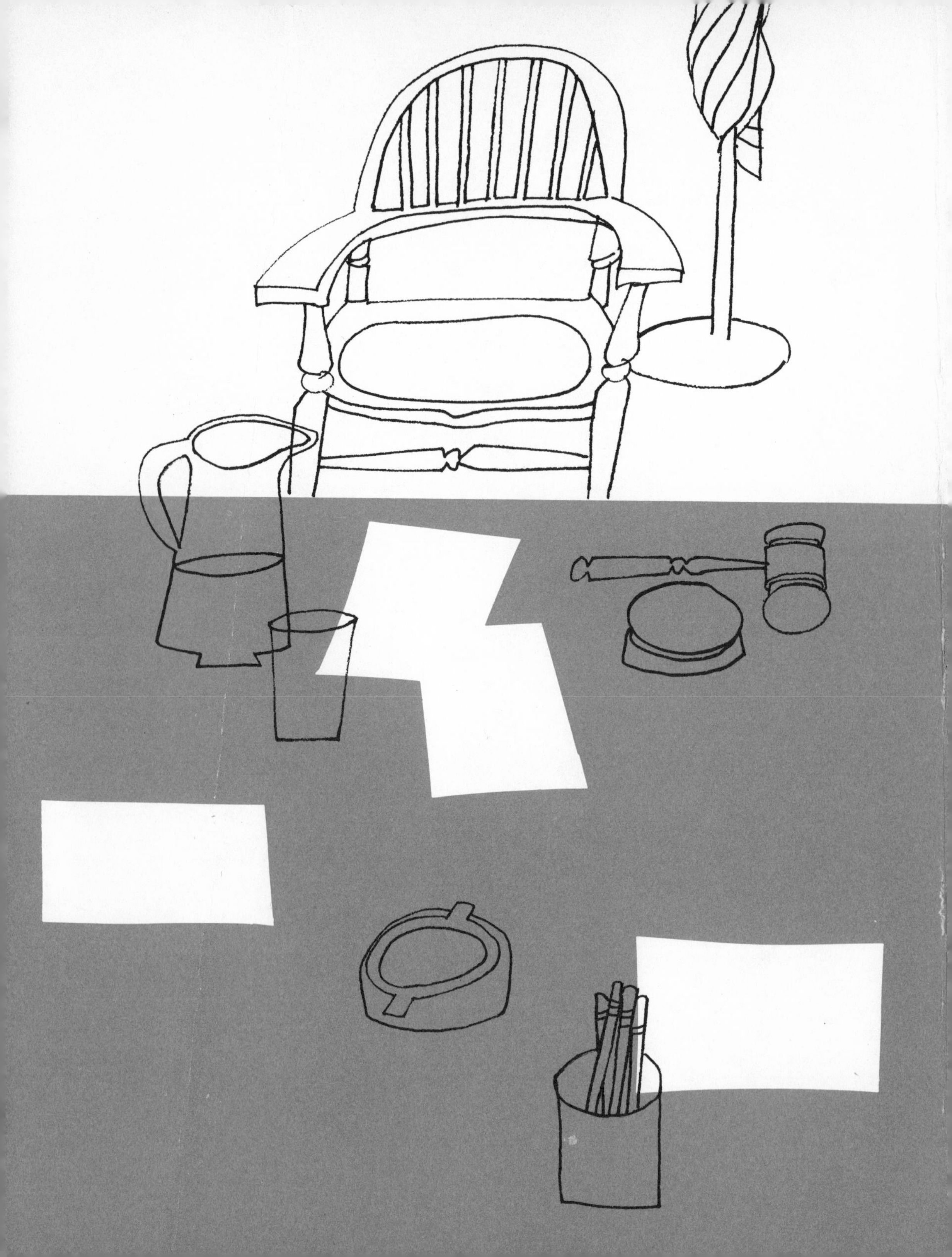

The FIRST BOOK of

HOW TO RUN A MEETING

by David Guy Powers

ILLUSTRATED BY PETER P. PLASENCIA

FRANKLIN WATTS, INC., 575 Lexington Ave., New York, N. Y. 10022

Library of Congress Catalog Card Number: 67-17556

Printed in the United States of America

1 2 3 4 5

CONTENTS

The FIRST BOOK of

HOW TO RUN A MEETING

YOU SELECT YOUR CLUBS

THE SELECTION of a club to join is like all the other choices you must make. You select a suit, a particular color, a dress, or even a bar of candy, according to your tastes. And you may prefer playing baseball to acting in a play; or you may like drawing pictures more than playing chess or singing a song. On the whole, you will find that you are happiest with people who have tastes similar to yours.

Some of the students in your school have the same interests you have. You will all find added pleasure in grouping together. The best way to do this is to join a club, or if there is none, to form one. You will find friends in the clubs of your school because clubs are based on the mutual interests of the members.

The wise thing to do is to select your clubs according to your deepest interests. Don't join too many, but be loyal to those you do join. Remember: Up to a point, each club will help you get more out of school life, but too many may waste your time.

Some of the most popular clubs are: Art; Aviation; Band; Cheerleaders; Chess; Cooking; Cycling; Drama; Electronics; Future Nurses of America; Glee Club; Good Grooming; Junior Red Cross; Languages (French, German, Spanish, or Classical); Library; Majorettes; Mathematics; Modern Dance; Nursing; Orchestra; Photography; Printing; Quill and Scroll (Creative Writing); Radio; Science; Sewing; Sports (Archery, Baseball, Basketball, Football, Swimming, Tennis); Television; Y Teens.

All these clubs hold meetings, and the meetings follow a set procedure, called *parliamentary procedure.* You will be happiest knowing the simple rules of this procedure. Learning the rules is not as difficult as it may seem. And once you have learned them, you will have added confidence in yourself.

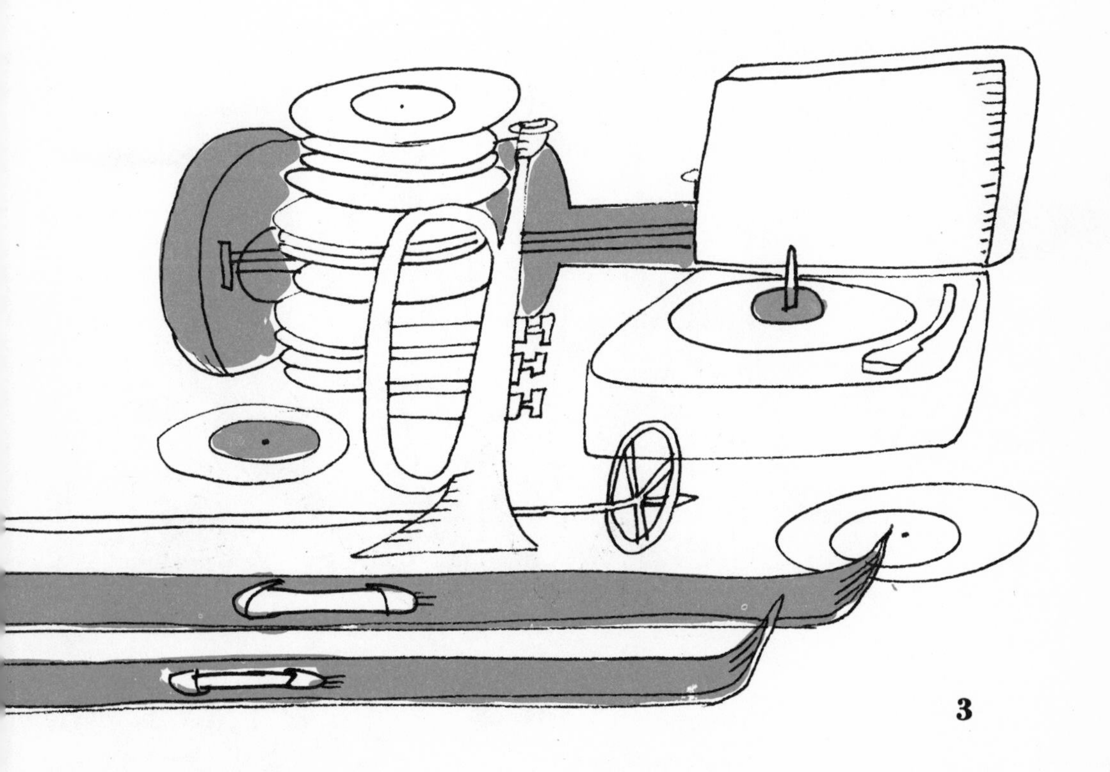

RULES OF CLUB PROCEDURE

THERE ARE four principles that are all-important to democracy, and they are all-important to the democratic running of your club. These principles are your guarantee of liberty. Learn them and live by them. They are as follows:

The wish of the majority must be followed.

You cannot always have your own way. You may want to go on a boat ride, and your friends may want to go on a hike. You cannot have a boat ride and a hike at the same time. As a member of a group, you have to "go along." You have to give a little to get a little.

Imagine what would happen if each of your fingers always went a separate way. Then you would never be able to use your hand. But each finger gains power when it acts as part of a team — a team called a hand.

The rights of the minority must be protected.

People see things from different angles. That is why there are so many paintings of the same subject. And that is why there are so many political parties. Sometimes you will find that you are in disagreement with the majority, and you will feel convinced that you are right. To feel this way is only human.

Parliamentary procedure in a group meeting assures that all members have a chance to express their opinions. Further, it assures their right to disagree. It is no disgrace to be in the minority. Often it is the role of bravery.

Respect for the dignity of all members must be assured.

You gain dignity by showing dignity to others. When you respect the rights of others you protect your own rights. When you are courteous you receive courtesy. When you listen attentively and treat other opinions with respect you will be listened to. Remember: Every member has rights equal to those of every other member.

When you become a club member you accept this contract. Membership means that you are willing to join a group of equal partners. Everyone has the same rights. To break this rule will make your club a fighting group. The club will get nothing done and will eventually break up.

Instead of this, work creatively to make friends; have the joy of getting things done; and reward yourself with the joyful experience of a club that is "great."

An order of business must be established.

The house that is in order, the person who is in order, and the daily program that is in order make for a happier life. In like manner, disorder creates distress and unhappiness among human beings.

In running a club, the need for order is important because a club involves many people. To be a good club member you must agree to follow a way of getting things done. Otherwise, the club will spend its time in endless wrangling. When you follow the four rules, you will get much more out of an active membership in your club.

The four rules to remember are:

1. The wish of the majority must be followed.
2. The rights of the minority must be protected.
3. Respect for the dignity of all members must be assured.
4. An order of business must be established.

HOW TO BECOME A GOOD CLUB MEMBER

WHEN you join a club, *really* join. Never be a halfhearted member. Agree to the rules and purposes of the group.

Ten guiding rules will help you gain the respect of your fellow club members.

1. Follow the rules agreed on by your club members.
2. Be polite to other members. Courtesy is priceless.
3. Put the good of the club first and your own wishes last.
4. When your idea is overruled, retire gracefully. Never sulk.

5. Remember: Good club members are those who go along with the group after a course of action has been decided on by the majority.
6. Seek every opportunity to serve.
7. At meetings, do not talk when someone else has the floor — that is, when a fellow member has been recognized by the chairman.
8. At meetings, always address the chairman by his title, "Mr. Chairman." When he calls your name, you have the floor and can speak without interruption.
9. At meetings, do not make a second proposal when another proposal is being discussed. Only one proposal, or motion, can be considered at a time.
10. Enjoy club meetings and enjoy getting things done.

HOW MEETINGS ARE CONDUCTED

The Chairman Presides

It is the privilege of the president of your club to preside at meetings. To "preside" means to be chairman and to follow an *agenda*, or order of business. There are eight steps to be taken in holding a meeting. The chairman should follow these. They are:

1. Call the meeting to order.
2. Hear the minutes of the previous meeting.
3. Hear reports of officers, boards, standing committees.
4. Hear reports of special committees.
5. Hear announcements.
6. Go on with the unfinished business of the last meeting.
7. Go on to new business.
8. End meeting (*adjourn*).

Write out these eight on a card, and you will be able to follow the meeting step by step.

1. Call the Meeting to Order

The chairman asks the secretary if enough members are present to have a meeting. If the answer is Yes, the chairman announces:

"The meeting will please come to order."

In order to hold a meeting, there must be a certain number of members present. In legislative bodies the number is usually "one more than half the members." In clubs this number is reduced to twenty per cent of the members. This is called a *quorum.* If there are not enough members present—*no quorum*—the chairman says:

"As there is no quorum, the meeting is adjourned."

The reason for this action is that a meeting with too few members present is not fair to all members. Any action taken might not be the true feeling of the club.

2. Hear the Minutes of the Previous Meeting

"Minutes" is a parliamentary word for the record of what happened at a previous meeting. To keep your club activities up to date, the members appoint a secretary to record the minutes. The secretary sets down the happenings at the meeting, and reports them at the beginning of the next meeting.

There are seven things to watch for in writing good minutes. Be sure the minutes include:

1. The name of the group.
2. The kind of meeting.
3. The place, date, and time of the meeting.
4. The name of the presiding officer.
5. Approval of the minutes of the previous meeting.
6. A list of the motions introduced, their proposers, and what finally happened — whether the proposal passed or failed.
7. The time of adjournment of the meeting.

Check your report against this list. If each item is covered, you will have an accurate report of the meeting. Good minutes tell who met, what they met for, who presided, when the meeting took place, where it took place, what happened, and the time when the meeting ended (adjourned).

Minutes are read by the secretary, after the chairman says:

"Will the secretary please read the minutes?"

After a satisfactory reading of the minutes, the chairman asks if there are any corrections. If there are none, he says:

"The minutes stand approved as read."

If corrections are suggested, the chairman instructs the secretary to make them. Should a difference of opinion arise, the chairman hears both sides and takes a vote.

"Shall the proposed correction be made? Those in favor say 'Aye.'" And after the Ayes, *"Those opposed say 'No.'"*

The group decides, and the chairman says:

"The corrections will be made [or not made] *and the minutes stand approved."*

3. Hear Reports of Officers, Boards, Standing Committees

As your club grows you will realize that large groups need small committees to help them. Committees spend time and study on a project and then report to the club.

Committee reports are simply advice to the club. The reports may be accepted or they may be rejected or they may be changed.

Some committees are appointed for the whole year or session. Others are appointed for special tasks — for instance, to find out where to hold the school dinner, or whether a certain gift is appropriate, or what books should be bought for the library.

The committees appointed for the entire year are called *standing committees*, and the task committees are called *special committees.*

A special committee has one task. When that task is finished, the committee goes out of existence; the members are dismissed with thanks.

Standing committees have year-long responsibilities. Later on in the book you will find a section on how committees work.

Committee recommendations are treated in two ways: The executive or standing committee reports are received as a matter of information, but the special committee reports are discussed as main motions.

4. Hear Reports of Special Committees

Special committees make reports to the club, and their recommendations are advisory to the club.

The reports may be accepted as reported; they may be revised by amendments; or they may be rejected by the club. They are like the advice of a friend. The club can follow the advice or merely thank the person giving the advice.

After the report has been made, the chairman says:

"You have heard the report of the committee. What is your pleasure?"

At this point the club members can enter the discussion. They can suggest changes, and they can make motions to accept or reject the committee report.

5. *Hear Announcements*

People love to know what's going on. Any event you plan needs to be known. A special time is allotted in a club meeting for telling people the news.

The chairman inquires:

"*Are there any announcements to be made at this time?*"

After the announcements have been made, there can be informal discussion and questions about them.

6. Go On with the Unfinished Business of the Last Meeting

Sometimes meetings are interrupted. Time runs out and everyone has to go to another place. The meeting must end, but what you were doing is left hanging in midair. The little chores that you postpone are called *unfinished business.*

In a club, everyone is unhappy if there are too many chores left undone. People are proud of themselves when their club is moving along. Because of this, a principle has grown up that you must finish one thing before you start another.

The rule is: *Always take up where you left off.*

Each meeting is a continuation of the last one. If you break this rule, your club will be scatterbrained and will lose members.

7. Go On to New Business

New business means exactly what it says. It is any suggestion for action not discussed before by the club.

It is wise, after a new plan has been suggested, to ask first for informal discussion. Any member can do this. The chairman has the privilege of suggesting a new proposal and may present his ideas. Then informal discussion takes place. The discussion is an exploration of the proposal. No one has to take sides. All members can freely express their views about the proposed action. Sometimes nothing comes of it and the matter is forgotten. The discussion has saved the club a good deal of time in the long run. And it has a bonus: Everyone has been allowed to speak on the proposal, or motion.

When the chairman feels that the discussion is complete, he asks: *"Does anyone desire to make a motion?"*

If no motion is made, the meeting is ready for any other proposal.

8. End Meeting (Adjourn)

When the business of the meeting is finished, the chairman says:

"If there is no further business, the meeting stands adjourned."

Any member may introduce a motion to adjourn at any time during the meeting, as long as he is not interrupting another speaker. He simply says:

"Mr. Chairman, I move we adjourn."

When the chairman hears the motion seconded, he says:

"It has been moved and seconded that the meeting adjourn."

Since a motion to adjourn is undebatable, the chairman immediately calls for a vote.

"All in favor of adjourning say 'Aye.'" After the Ayes, *"Those opposed, 'No.'"*

If the Ayes have it, *"The motion is carried. The meeting stands adjourned."*

If the motion is lost by a majority of votes of No, the meeting continues. The motion to adjourn can be remade after a reasonable time.

If a motion is being debated at the time of adjournment, it comes up as unfinished business at the next regular meeting of the club.

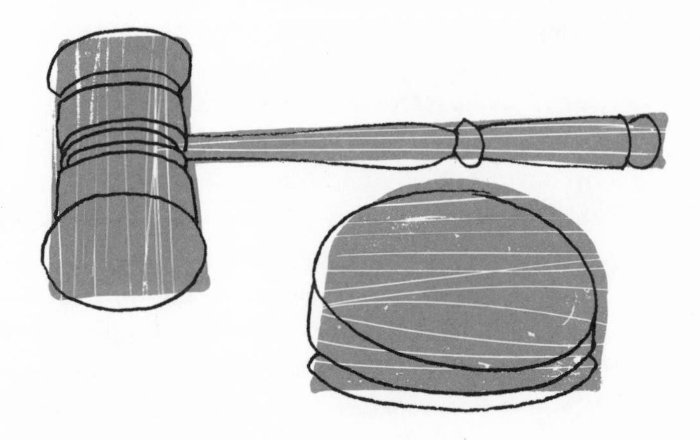

MOTIONS—VARIOUS KINDS

A MOTION is a way of getting your idea before the group. In order to do this, you must know the rules. Once you know them, you will find that making a motion is a simple matter.

How To Make a Motion

A proposal for action is made in the form of a motion. For the group to consider the motion, at least two members must be in favor of it. The first member makes the motion. The second member seconds the motion, to show his approval.

Motions should be expressed in an affirmative manner — that is, they should suggest that the club do something, rather than that it *not* do something. The following is an example of a main motion:

"I move that the club donate ten dollars to Boys Town."

How To Present a Motion

There are eight simple steps in presenting a main motion:

1. The member rises and addresses the Chair (the chairman).
2. The member is recognized by the Chair.
3. The member states his proposal.
4. Another member seconds the motion.
5. The motion is restated by the Chair.
6. The chairman conducts the discussion.
7. The chairman puts the question to a vote.
8. The chairman announces the result.

The main motion forms the starting point for any action to be taken by the group. Informal discussion may be allowed in small groups, but to be considered, the motion must be *made, seconded,* and *stated by the chairman.*

The chairman should know the exact moment at which to stop any informal discussion. He may bring things to a head by saying:

"If definite action is sought in this matter, a motion is in order."

This is how a motion is made:

1. Stand and address the chairman: *"Mr. Chairman"* or *"Mr. President."* Wait until you are recognized by the chairman. Do not speak until you are recognized by a nod or by name: "Edward."
2. Be sure you have your motion clearly in mind, and worded as briefly as possible. Write it out if you can.
3. When you have been recognized, state the motion so that all can hear:
   "I move that this club give a rising vote of thanks to its sponsor, Dr. Smith."
4. After the motion has been made, another member, without waiting to be recognized, calls out:
   "I second the motion."

5. The motion having been made and seconded, the chairman states the motion by saying:
"It has been moved and seconded that this club give a rising vote of thanks to its sponsor, Dr. Smith."
6. When the chairman has stated the motion, it is said to be pending. It may now be considered by the group—that is, it is open to discussion and debate.
7. Any member may now rise to agree or disagree with the proposal. For example, a member may rise and say: *"Mr. Chairman."* The chairman says: "Betsy," so giving her permission to speak.
"I agree with the motion. Dr. Smith has given his time to us and we should express our gratitude to him."
8. The chairman inquires:
"Is there any further discussion?"
Since no one rises to discuss the motion further, the chairman asks:
"Are you ready for the question?" (The "question" is the vote.)
The members call out, *"Question!"*
The response, "Question," is a parliamentary form which shows that the members are ready to vote. It is similar to another traditional response, "Hear, Hear!" which means that members agree with the speaker.
9. The chairman then puts the question—that is, he takes the vote. He says:
"It has been moved and seconded that this club give a rising vote of thanks to its sponsor, Dr. Smith. All those in favor of the motion say 'Aye.'"
The members in favor of the motion say, "Aye."
The chairman then says:
"Those opposed, say 'No.'"
The members who disapprove of the motion then say, "No."

10. The chairman then announces the vote:
"The Ayes have it. The motion is carried." Or, *"The Noes have it. The motion is defeated."*

Kinds of Motions

There are four kinds of motions:

Privileged motions
Subsidiary motions
Incidental motions
Main motions

Motions that concern the rights and privileges of members are called *privileged motions.* Because of their urgency and importance they come before all other motions. The most common privileged motions are:

1. To fix time and place for adjournment.
2. To adjourn.
3. To take a recess.
4. Matters of personal privilege.
5. Orders of the day.

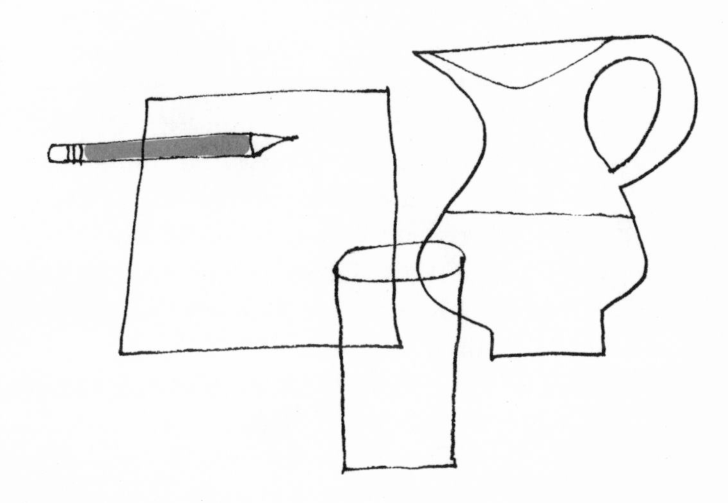

You will notice that four of these motions concern general rights. They are the rights reserved to the group: when to adjourn, when to recess, and when to insist that the rules be followed. The other motion, the motion of privilege, is the most important. It refers to a member's individual and personal rights.

Let us take an example of how this motion actually works.

Whenever there is any disturbance to the group, such as noise, presence of non-members, quarrels between members, or unpleasant atmospheric conditions, like excessive heat or cold, you may rise to a question of privilege. Suppose there is so much noise that you cannot hear. You might stand, and without waiting to be recognized, say:

"Mr. Chairman, I rise to a point of personal privilege."

The chairman would then tell you to state your point of privilege. You might say, "There is too much noise. I can't hear."

Motions of personal privilege require no second, and are immediately decided by the chairman. In this case, he might direct the speaker to talk more loudly or he might take some other measure, such as closing the windows to shut out the disturbance. Business would then be resumed.

Such a privileged motion enables you to secure your rights. It should not be used for a trifling matter, however, because it does interrupt the business of the meeting.

Subsidiary motions amend or otherwise dispose of other motions. There are seven of them. The two you may want to use, however, are: (1) to refer to a committee, and (2) to amend.

You use the refer-to-a-committee motion whenever you feel that the group should study the proposition more carefully before voting on it. You rise and say, *"Mr. Chairman."*

When recognized, you then say:

"I move that this question be referred to a committee."

This motion must be seconded. It can be amended. It can be

debated. It cannot be reconsidered once the committee has begun its study. It requires a majority vote.

The motion to amend seeks to modify or change the motion under consideration. When you wish to make it, you must rise and say, "*Mr. Chairman.*"

When you have been recognized by the chairman, you might say, "*I move to amend the motion by striking out the word 'annual.'*"

When you make this motion, you must be sure to state definitely the way in which you want the amendment made. (See page 24 for more about amendments.)

Motions that arise out of debate are called *incidental motions.* They are concerned with small matters that can readily be settled. For example, a member desires to know some matter of information (point of information), or a member desires to question a vote (divide the assembly), or a member desires to know if the proper procedure is being followed (point of order).

A *main motion* brings a new proposal before the club. It is only in order when no other main motion is being debated.

A main motion is subject to six conditions:

1. It must be seconded.
2. It can be amended.
3. It can be debated.
4. It can be reconsidered — that is, brought up a second time.
5. It can have additional motions that change it.
6. It requires a majority vote.

On page 58 a Simplified Chart is provided to show you the four types of motions. The chart also shows you the purpose of each motion. It should be extremely valuable to you as you use it. It will give you the ready answer to many questions.

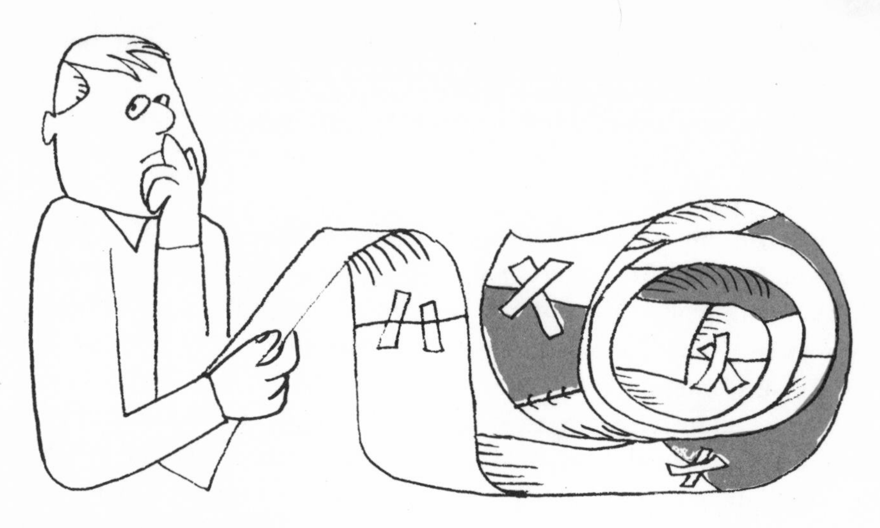

AMENDMENTS

IN PARLIAMENTARY PROCEDURE a proposal for action is called a motion. Often the motion does not indicate what the group really wants to do, so a system has developed to get nearer to the group's wishes. This is a system of *amendments.* An amendment is the means by which an original proposal is changed.

Four Types of Amendments

There are four standard ways of amending, or changing:

1. Amending by *striking out.*
2. Amending by *inserting.*
3. Amending by *dividing the motion* into two motions.
4. Amending by *substituting.*

These changes are similar to correcting a sentence. You amend the sentence to make it mean exactly what you have in mind. A group must do the same thing. The members must work together to get the motion to express their wishes. They can strike out words in the original amendment; they can insert words; they can add words; they can substitute words. In this way the proposal, or motion, can be changed so that it will receive the full cooperation of all members.

The form is:

"I move to amend the main motion by [state change]."

The chairman conducts the discussion, and then says:

"All in favor of the amendment to [here he states the change] *say 'Aye.'"*

Then:

"All those opposed say 'No.'

"The Ayes have it, and the amendment is carried."

The chairman reads the motion as amended.

Amendments can go only to the second degree. For example, the main motion is proposed.

"I move that the club donate twenty-five dollars to Boys Town."

A motion can be made to amend the main motion by striking out "twenty-five dollars" and inserting "fifteen dollars." An amendment of the amendment can be proposed that "fifteen dollars" be stricken out and "ten dollars" inserted.

To illustrate this point:

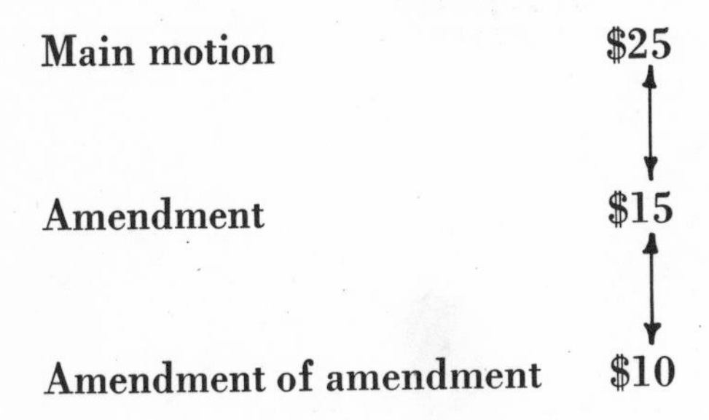

To amend further would be a third degree of amendment. The "ten dollars" amendment cannot be changed.

That is how amendments are made. They begin with the making

of the main motion, and they proceed step by step to full discussion of each amendment.

Step 1: The main motion is made, seconded, and opened for debate.

Step 2: An amendment is made, seconded, and opened for debate.

Step 3: An amendment of the amendment is made, seconded, and opened for debate.

No other amendment can be allowed.

An easy way to remember the two types of amendments is:

1. When the amendment seeks to change the main motion, it is called an amendment of the first rank.
2. When the amendment seeks to change another amendment, it is called an amendment of the second rank.

3. There cannot be such a thing as an amendment of the third rank. It would lead to endless confusion.

Here is a chart that shows how a well-regulated meeting considers our proposal. The main motion is proposed:

"I move that the club donate twenty-five dollars to Boys Town."

A member makes an amendment:

"I move to strike out twenty-five dollars and insert fifteen dollars."

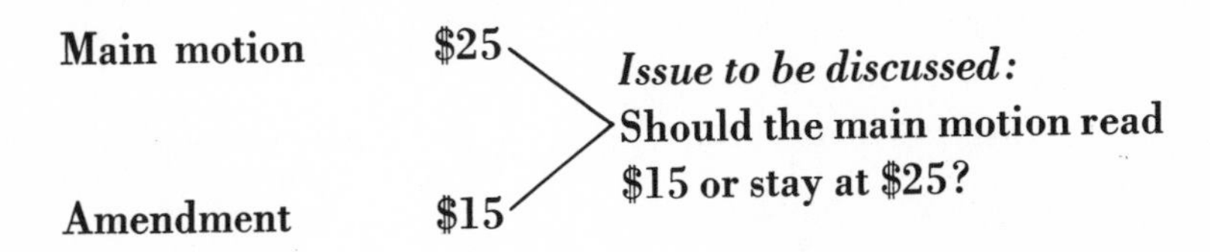

After full debate, the chairman suggests that the group vote. When this is agreed to without dissent, he says:

"It has been moved and seconded that twenty-five dollars be stricken out, and fifteen dollars be inserted. Those in favor say 'Aye.' "

Then:

"Those opposed say 'No.' "

The vote of the majority decides whether the main motion now reads "twenty-five dollars" or "fifteen dollars." If the amendment carries by a majority vote, the main motion reads "fifteen dollars." The main motion has now become:

"The club shall donate fifteen dollars to Boys Town."

Discussion is now in order. All members may debate whether or not they wish to donate the fifteen dollars to Boys Town. After full debate, the members have the chance to vote Yes or No on the motion.

The above example represents the use of an amendment of the first rank. In brief, a motion was made, an amendment was offered, the amendment carried, and the group voted on the motion that was changed. This example is the simplest form of the process of amendment.

An amendment of the second rank follows.

There may be a feeling that fifteen dollars is more than the club can afford. Some members may think that ten dollars is preferable. In that case, any member has the right to make a motion of the second rank — namely, to reduce the fifteen dollars to ten dollars. He makes a motion to amend the amendment. *He must make this before the amendment of the first rank has been settled.*

The member rises, is recognized by the chairman, and says:

"I move to amend the amendment by striking out fifteen dollars and inserting ten dollars."

When his motion is seconded, and stated by the chairman, the following chart applies:

Amendment	$15	*Issue to be discussed:* Should the amendment read $10 or stay at $15?
Amendment of amendment	$10	

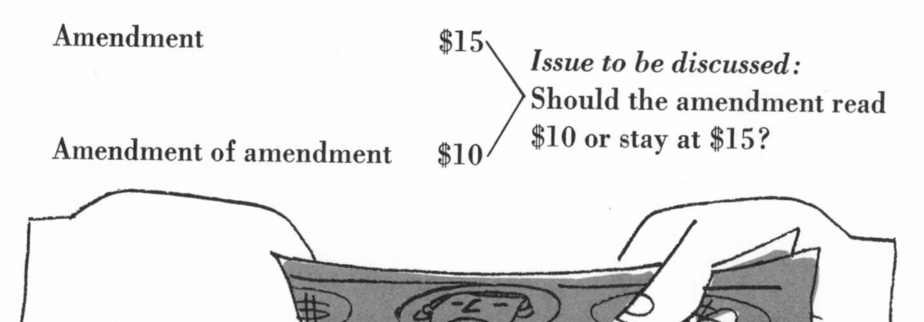

The chairman limits debate to the preference of ten dollars over fifteen dollars. No other matter is in order. After full debate, the chairman suggests that the group vote. When this is agreed to without dissent, he says:

"It has been moved and seconded that fifteen dollars be stricken out, and ten dollars be inserted. Those in favor say 'Aye.'"

Then:

"Those opposed say 'No.'"

Skillful Use of Amendments

To secure action, the chairman must now move in a manner that seems backward. Every amendment has to be settled before a final action is taken on the main motion. The reason is that amendments are a means of getting the main motions in shape. *When a main motion expresses the wish of the majority of club members it has the best chance of passing.*

So, the procedure of voting is the reverse of the way amendments were presented:

Step 1: The amendment of the amendment is first put to vote.

Step 2: The amendment is then put to vote.

Step 3: The main motion is finally put to vote.

The reason the voting is reversed is that you must decide the changes in the main motion before you can vote for it or against it.

For example, let us assume the victory of each amendment. In the vote of the "ten dollars" against the "fifteen dollars" amendment the vote was favorable. So the amendment now reads "ten dollars." This must be debated against the main motion of twenty-five dollars.

After full debate the amendment carried, and the main motion now reads "ten dollars." The club then votes on the main motion of ten dollars.

This is the way the debate and voting would go:

Amendment of amendment	$10	Choice voted on first
against	or	
Amendment	$15	

The majority decides $10 is better.

Amendment	$10	Choice voted on second
against	or	
Main motion	$25	

The majority decides $10 is better.

Main motion	$10	Choice — Yes or No — voted on this

The club now approves or rejects by a majority vote the motion to contribute ten dollars.

While the system of amendments may seem like a slow process, it is the most fair. It permits every club member to have his say. And in the long run it gets the best results.

Germane or Not?

There is one restriction on an amendment: it must be *germane.* A germane amendment is one that without any doubt has something to do with the main proposal. A motion to raise the dues could be amended by striking out "to raise" and inserting "to lower." While the amendment is hostile to the main motion, it is still germane to it.

A motion to go on an outing could be amended by adding, "and take a boat trip up the river." This amendment is germane, since it proposes something having directly to do with the outing. The motion to go on an outing could not be amended by adding "and to elect a new secretary," however. This amendment is not germane — it has nothing to do with the motion — and therefore it would be out of order. In such case the chairman says:

"Since this amendment is not germane to the main motion, it is out of order."

SPECIAL COMMITTEES

ONE of the most useful devices for carrying on club business is the *special committee.* Such a committee is a means of gathering information that may guide the group. For example, your club may be debating a motion, and gradually the members realize that they do not have enough information on it. They are puzzled. No one at the meeting has the facts. In such a case the intelligent thing to do is to choose a few people to find out the facts.

This is what a special committee is. It is a group chosen to find out the necessary information. The chairman appoints several members — usually three, but always an odd number. They set to work and at the next meeting they report their findings. Their report gives the club members important information, and the committee's recommendations help the club decide just what it wants to do.

Any member may move to refer a proposal to a committee. And when the member's motion is seconded by another member and receives a majority vote, the chairman must appoint such a committee.

Special committees are so called because each is assigned to study one special action. The committee goes out of existence after it reports back to the group. In parliamentary language it is called an *ad hoc* committee. *Ad hoc* is Latin, meaning "for this purpose alone."

This is how a member makes a motion to appoint a committee:

"Mr. Chairman, I move that this motion be assigned to a special committee."

Another member says (and he does not need to be recognized by the chairman):

"I second the motion."

After the motion to appoint a committee has been passed by a majority vote, the chairman selects the committee. Should the member making the motion wish to indicate either the number of members or the names of the committee members, he would make the motion in this form:

"Mr. Chairman, I move that the motion be referred to a committee of three to be appointed by the Chair."

or,

"Mr. Chairman, I move that the motion be referred to a committee of three: namely, Edward, James, and Sarah."

The member making the motion for a special committee has still another privilege. He may indicate the time at which the committee must report its findings. For example, he may move:

"Mr. Chairman, I move that the motion be referred to a committee appointed by the Chair, with the instructions to report their recommendations at the next regular meeting."

The motion can be changed as to the *number on the committee* and the *time* at which the report is due. These changes are offered as amendments. In other words, the number of members on the committee can be altered, and the time to report can be altered, but the appointment of the committee *must* go to a vote by all members.

STANDING COMMITTEES

A STANDING COMMITTEE is chosen for the time during which the appointing body lasts — that is, for the term of the club officers. It is different from a special committee in that it does not go out of existence after it reports. Its business continues through the session, and its reports bring the group up to date on its (the committee's) activities. The chairman may appoint the whole committee or he may appoint a committee chairman who then selects the other members.

Standing committees do the solid work of the club. Much business is shifted to them throughout the year. Because these committees "stand," and do not go out of existence, the whole club is assured that certain tasks will be carried out regularly. Such continuing tasks as collecting and spending money, recruiting new members, and revising bylaws are the work of some of the usual standing committees.

All standing committees make annual reports. During the year, however, a subject can be withdrawn from a standing committee by a majority vote. This is usually done when a matter in committee becomes urgent and needs immediate and special attention.

There are five standing committees that clubs have found most useful: the membership committee, the finance committee, the house committee, the educational committee, and the program committee.

The Membership Committee

This committee has the responsibility of executing the rules governing the good standing of members, and of searching for ways and means of attracting desirable new members. The membership committee has been called the lifeline of a club. In large part it determines the tone of the present membership, and fashions the future membership by its decisions. By strictly and honorably applying the intent of the constitution, it preserves the character of the club. It may also make recommendations to the group for changes in the rules of admission and may report its decision on questionable applications.

The Finance Committee

This committee is responsible for safeguarding and spending the money of the club. Usually the club's treasurer is the chairman of the committee. All recommendations for changes in dues, for building expenditures, for sales, and for any other money matter are referred to this committee for consideration.

The House Committee

This committee has power to administer the physical equipment, personnel, and food owned by the organization. The tasks include general upkeep of the club properties and arrangement for special events and banquets.

The Educational Committee

This committee is charged with programming educational events of interest to the members. In some types of clubs it handles such items as art exhibits, arts and crafts, dramatic reviews, and book discussions.

The Program Committee

This committee arranges the weekly or monthly entertainments. The duties vary from group to group, but generally the committee determines the nature of the set programs given at regular meetings. Great care should be taken in selecting this committee.

In planning programs it is wise to seek the advice of a faculty member and enlist the aid of other teachers and other clubs. It is quite easy to find other clubs with common interests, and they will cooperate in programs. Beware of overplanning, but do have programs that are interesting to everyone. Above all, use your librarian. He or she will be a great help to you in finding material and planning exciting programs.

HOW TO MAKE A COMMITTEE REPORT

A COMMITTEE REPORT should start with a clear statement of the problem referred to the committee. Next, it should state the way the investigation was carried on, and finally it should make its recommendations. Committee reports are made orally by the committee chairman. For example, if a committee has been appointed merely to find out some information, the committee chairman presents the facts to the club. The chairman expresses the club's gratitude for a job well done. This is the simplest type of committee report.

The chairman of a special committee — one appointed for a specific problem only — must be prepared to answer any questions of the club members. A member rises and addresses the chairman thus:

"Mr. Chairman, I rise to a point of information."

The chairman responds:

"State your point of information."

The chairman listens to the inquiry and requests the committee chairman to answer. He should be prepared to do so. If not, he refers the question to another member of his committee. In all instances the situation should be one of friendly help and cooperation.

Committee reports should have specific recommendations. It is the committee's duty to study the proposal assigned to it and reach a decision. The most important item of the report is a clear recommendation.

For example, the chairman of the committee assigned to investigate where the spring outing of the class should be held may end his report by saying: "The committee respectfully suggests that the spring outing be a boat ride to West Point."

The club chairman responds:

"You have heard the recommendation of the committee. What is your pleasure?"

The recommendation of the committee becomes a main motion. It is open to amendment by the club members. Any changes they wish may be made through the process of amendments. Usually such committee reports are strongly supported by the club and are gratefully received and followed.

HOW VOTES ARE TAKEN

The Chair Takes a Vote

A vote is the means by which the group makes decisions. Voting is done in the following manner:

1. One member puts the action before the club by making a motion, which is seconded by another member.

2. The chairman states the motion, which is now open for consideration by the group.

3. After enough time has been allowed for discussion, the chairman puts the question. He asks those in favor of the motion to respond by saying "Aye." Those opposed are asked to respond by saying "No." The chairman evaluates the votes and announces the result.

"The Ayes have it and the motion is carried."

or

"The Noes have it and the motion is defeated."

This procedure is called taking the vote, or putting the question.

General Consent

General consent is a method of voting that saves time and speeds matters up. It can be used in the handling of routine business, of matters of slight importance, and of proposals on which the wish of the group is quite clear.

The approval of the reading of the minutes of the previous meeting furnishes an example of a routine matter that can be accomplished by use of general consent. After the minutes have been read, the chairman asks:

"*Are there any corrections or additions?*"

After a brief pause, he may then say:

"*Since there are no corrections or additions, the minutes stand as read.*"

If an objection is raised, this method cannot be used. It must be discarded and a vote taken.

Viva Voce (*Voiced Vote*)

A voiced vote is the most common and the easiest way of taking the opinion of the group. The chairman states the proposal to the club, and then says:

"*All those in favor say 'Aye.'* "

When he has heard their response, he says:

"*All those opposed say 'No.'* "

By the volume of the response he can determine which side has the greater number of votes. He then announces the results. Any member who doubts the chairman's decision may request a recount by a show of hands or a standing vote.

Show of Hands

In this method the members indicate their vote by raising their right hands. The chairman says:

"*All those in favor, please raise your right hand.*"

When these have been counted by the secretary, the chairman says:

"*Those opposed, please raise your right hand.*"

These are counted and the chairman announces the results.

"The Ayes have it and the motion is carried."

or

"The Noes have it and the motion is defeated."

Rising, or Standing, Vote

In most cases a vote by voice or by a show of hands will do. If there is any doubt of the results, however, the chairman calls for a rising vote. He says:

"Those in favor of the motion please rise and be counted."

After these have been counted, he says:

"Be seated. Those opposed to the motion, please rise."

The chairman and the secretary count the votes, or the chairman may direct tellers to do so.

After the count has been taken, the chairman states the number of votes for and the number of votes against the motion and announces the result.

If the chairman does not call for a rising vote, any member may do so by saying:

"I call for a division."

This need not be seconded and cannot be debated. The chairman calls for a rising vote. This must be understood as a request from a member who feels that the previous vote has been in error. The chairman readily agrees to this request. He simply announces:

"A call for a division has been made, and the vote will be retaken."

Members should use this privilege with caution. It can easily waste time and make group action difficult.

Roll Call

A roll-call vote is a permanent record of the way in which each member voted.

The chairman announces:

"The secretary will now call the roll. Each member will answer 'Aye' or 'No' as his name is called."

The secretary calls the roll. As his name is called each member rises and answers "Aye" or "No." If he does not wish to vote, he responds, "Present." The secretary records these answers in separate columns.

After the roll call has been completed, the secretary reads the names of those who voted in the affirmative, then of those who voted in the negative, and finally the names of those who voted Present. This allows a chance for mistakes to be corrected. The chairman announces the result of the roll-call vote.

Ballot

When a secret vote is wished, the ballot method of voting is used. This method should be used for elections, acceptance of new members, and punishment of members by means of disciplinary actions. When the vote to be taken can be expressed by yes or no, the secretary provides slips of paper for this purpose. The chairman then appoints tellers to distribute the slips to the members. After making certain that each member has received a ballot, the chairman directs the members to vote yes or no. After each member has done so, the tellers collect the ballots and tally the results.

The chairman gives the signal for the announcement of the results.

The chief teller reads the results. He then gives his report to the secretary. This report indicates:

1. The number of votes cast.
2. The number of votes for and the number against.
3. The number of illegal ballots and the reason for their rejection.

The chairman then announces the results as follows:

"Sixty votes were cast for the office of [here he states office]. *Thomas received forty-two votes, Susan received sixteen votes, and two ballots were declared illegal since they were cast for candidates not nominated for this office. The new duly elected* [he states office] *is Thomas."*

Since balloting takes a good deal of time, it is best to avoid the ballot form if possible. Save it for the situations definitely mentioned in the club's constitution or bylaws. Any member has the right to request a written ballot, however, when in his judgment it is in the best interest of the club. This can easily be settled by the chairman. He says:

"A request has been made to conduct this vote by ballot. Is there any objection to this procedure? There being none, the Chair will appoint tellers."

This procedure assumes a unanimous vote, since there was no objection. When the request is made as a motion and seconded, the chairman immediately takes a voiced vote, since the motion cannot be debated or amended.

Tellers

The chairman has the privilege of selecting the tellers — that is, the counters of the votes. The first-named teller is the chief teller. The chief teller divides the members into groups and assigns a teller to each group. In the case of a standing vote or a rising vote this is quite simple, and assigning the tellers speeds up the business of the meeting. In like manner, when there is a written ballot the chief teller assigns each assistant to an area and supervises the distribution and collection of the ballots. Instructions for voting may be given by the chairman or the chief teller.

After the ballots have been collected they are counted by the tellers with the assistance of the secretary. The secretary or chief teller tallies the results as the tellers indicate them. The chief teller then tabulates the ballots and advises the chairman of the results.

Tellers do not lose their own right to vote. When a voiced or standing vote is used, they indicate their choice to the chief teller. When a written form is used, they submit a ballot to the chief teller at the time of collection. Care should be taken to be as formal as possible in conducting the vote and counting the ballots, for endless bickering can result when there is a question of inaccuracy.

In announcing the results, the chairman must make known to the members the full facts of the voting. When the vote is overwhelming in one direction, the chairman may show his consideration by merely announcing the prevailing side. But when the matter of ruling out ballots, of ineligible ballots, or of a wide number of blanks arises, it is wise so to inform the members.

In strict parliamentary procedure — especially in the matter of the election of candidates to office — the exact number of votes received by each candidate, the number of rejected ballots, together with the reasons for their rejection, and the number of blank votes cast must be announced and made part of the record. This action assures the right of appeal and is a basic democratic heritage.

In club meetings the ballot form is used principally for nominations and important changes in the structure of the club. In such situations the procedure should be businesslike and fair, and should reflect in every way the desire of the chairman to carry out the will of the entire group.

HOW TO CONDUCT ELECTIONS

THE MOST important action of your group is the election of its officers. This matter should be given the utmost care and attention. The decisions made in an election determine the future of your club. The selection of good leaders means success, while the election of poor leaders means failure. Think long and hard about the candidates you nominate.

In the constitution and bylaws of your club there are probably definite directions for the election of officers. The chairman should see to it that these directions are carried out. If your constitution gives no such directions, any member may propose a motion suggesting the means of electing officers. The following methods have been found to be the most effective.

Nominations by Committee

Some months before the election date, the president may appoint a nominating committee. Or any member may introduce a motion to have such a committee selected by the group. The committee's purpose is to present to the club members a slate of nominees — a list of candidates — for the various offices. Names for the list may be suggested to the committee by any member. Such a committee should not be rushed. It should study the candidates and should find out if they are willing to serve.

At the appointed time, the chairman calls for the report of the nominating committee. The committee chairman presents his report:

"Mr. Chairman, the nominating committee wishes to submit the following slate:

"1. For president, Mr. Robert Townsend.

"2. For vice-president, Mr. Andrew Wilson.

"3. For secretary, Miss Janet Reed.

"4. For treasurer, Mr. Thomas Hart."

The presentation of the slate does not mean election. The club members at the meeting have the right to make additions to the slate. If none are made, the chairman inquires:

"You have heard the proposed slate of the committee. What is your pleasure?"

If the group is ready to vote, the chairman puts the question:

"All those in favor of the submitted slate say 'Aye.'" Then: *"The officers have been duly elected."*

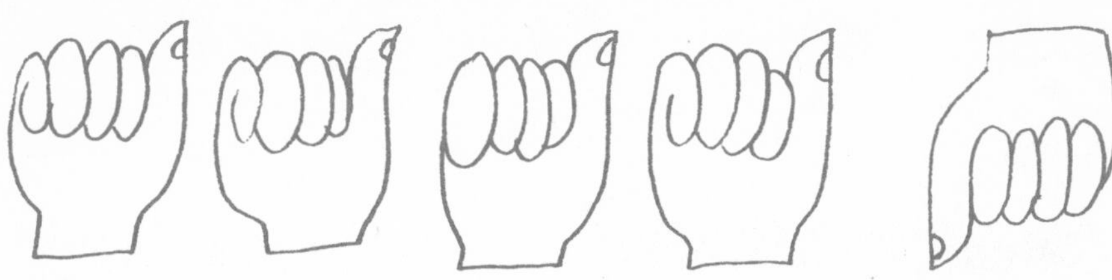

Often, as a form of courtesy, a member moves to make the selection unanimous. If no objection is voiced, the chairman instructs the secretary to cast a single ballot for the slate. This makes the election of all officers unanimous. It cannot be done if there is any objection by a member.

Nominations from the Floor

This method of nominating is less formal. It is used in many small groups. The chairman informs the members that nominations are in order as follows:

"*Nominations are in order for the office of* [names the office]."

A member rises, is recognized, and states:

"*Mr. Chairman, I nominate James Scott for president.*"

The chairman receives the nomination and states:

"*Mr. James Scott has been nominated for president. Are there any further nominations for this office?*"

Members may continue to nominate for this office. When the chairman feels that all members have had enough time, he inquires:

"*Are there any objections to closing the nominations for president? There being none, the nominations are closed.*"

The same procedure is used for the nomination of the other officers. Nominations need not be seconded, but they do not hold unless they are accepted by the nominee. If he declines the nomination, his name must be withdrawn.

Nominating Speeches

There may be brief nominating speeches. These are best limited to two minutes, and should not be made by more than two members. In making such a speech, it is wise to state simply why you believe the candidate you place in nomination will benefit the club.

Closing Nominations

This may be done in two ways: (1) the chairman may declare nominations closed if there is no objection; or (2) any member may make a motion to close the nominations. The usual procedure is that the chairman asks:

"Are there any further nominations for the office of president? The Chair hears none. Nominations for that office are closed and we will proceed to election."

Nominations may be reopened by a motion from any member. It is not debatable, and requires a majority vote. This is to protect the group from any hasty action by the chairman. It is rarely needed.

Elections

Because of the personal nature of the elections, it is best that they be held by secret ballot. (See page 42, *Ballot.*) This preserves your right as a member to the privacy of your choice, and it also protects the candidates from embarrassment.

When there is only one candidate proposed for an office, the chairman can declare him elected without balloting. More than one candidate for a position requires the use of the written ballot. Unless otherwise stated in the constitution, a majority (one more than half) elects the candidate. If there is a tie vote, the chairman may cast the deciding vote. He cannot do so if he has previously joined in the regular voting. In such a case, additional elections are held until a majority vote is received by one candidate.

When more than one office is to be filled, it is easiest to hold separate balloting for each post. In all cases the counting of the votes is done by the tellers. (See page 43: *Tellers.*)

RULES TO LIVE BY

The Constitution

EVERY GROUP succeeds best when it abides by self-selected rules. Such rules must be approved by the majority after full discussion, and they are binding on all the members. To give your group a good start, frame a set of principles to guide you.

This is simple if you restrict your constitution to six basic items: (1) the name of the club; (2) the purpose of the club (what your group wants to do); (3) the requirements for membership (the type of person you think should belong); (4) the officers and how to elect them; (5) the time and place of meetings; (6) the ways of changing any of the above by amendments.

The Bylaws

Other rules that are more specific than the constitution are called bylaws. They are more easily changed and make it easier to run the club smoothly. Again, six simple items will save endless discussion and avoid many arguments: (1) spell out how long the officers should stay in office and what authority they will have; (2) name the permanent (standing) committees and their purposes; (3) decide on dues, fines, and the method of paying bills; (4) decide the date for elections and the time at which they should be held; (5) decide how meetings should be conducted; (6) select the quorum — the number of the membership that must be present to begin a meeting. Ten to twenty per cent of the members is the wisest choice for a quorum.

Make your constitution and bylaws easy to accept but difficult to change. For example, adopt them by majority vote — one more than half the members present and voting — and permit them to be changed only by a two-thirds (2/3) vote. This will give a solid foundation to your club organization, and it will prevent many of the petty changes that cause squabbles and arguments.

Sample Constitution and Bylaws

CONSTITUTION

ARTICLE I

The name of this club shall be The Forest Hills Drama Club.

ARTICLE II

Purpose

The purpose of this organization shall be the fostering of interest in all the forms of dramatic art. This includes the theater, acting, oral reading of poetry, and the production and seeing of plays in our school and community.

ARTICLE III

Membership

Membership shall be open to all students who show a sincere interest in the dramatic arts: those who appear in school plays; those who demonstrate ability in reading poetry; those who assist in the production of plays; and those who regularly attend community plays.

ARTICLE IV

Officers

The officers of this drama club shall consist of a president, a vice-president, a secretary, and a treasurer who shall be elected at the third last meeting of each school year.

ARTICLE V

Meetings

Regular meetings shall be held in the free hour each week on Tuesdays at 12 noon during the school year. Special meetings may be called by the president, or by the petition of any ten members.

ARTICLE VI

Amendment

Amendment shall be by a three-fourths (3/4) vote of the total active membership. Notice shall be given at the regular meeting preceding the meeting at which action is to be voted.

BYLAWS

Officers' Term of Office

Officers shall be elected at the third last meeting of each school year. They shall be nominated from the floor, and a majority vote shall elect. The term of office shall be one year. The vice-president, the secretary, and the treasurer shall remain in office during the tenure of the president.

Committees

The president shall appoint the following committees each year:

1. A membership committee, consisting of five members.
2. A finance committee, to collect and expend money.
3. A house committee, to supervise all physical properties.
4. A social committee, to arrange all the performances.
5. A program committee, representing each of the dramatic arts.

Dues

The dues shall be fifty cents per semester. Anyone failing to pay his dues will be notified by the secretary. Failure to pay by the next regular meeting means dismissal. Any special dues shall only be levied by a two-thirds (2/3) vote of the members. Any member absenting himself from a regular meeting for two or more successive meetings shall be fined twenty-five (25) cents.

Date for Elections

Elections shall be held at the third last meeting of the school year.

Parliamentary Authority

All questions not covered in the constitution or these bylaws shall be resolved by Powers, *Parliamentary Procedure* (Data-Guide, New York, 1964).

Quorum

One-fifth (1/5) of the active members of this club shall be a quorum. In the absence of a quorum no meeting can be held.

Amendment

These bylaws may be amended by a two-thirds (2/3) vote of the members present and voting. The proposed change must be announced at the previous regular meeting, however.

Approval by Members

The chairman of the club presents the constitution and bylaws to the members for approval, called ratification. This should be done by first reading the entire document, and then considering one section at a time. (This is called *seriatim.*) As each section is read it is debated, and if any change is necessary it is made by majority vote. Usually there is little correction to be made. After everyone has had a fair chance to voice his opinion, ratification of the constitution is put to a vote by the chairman and carried by a majority vote.

THE LANGUAGE OF MEETING PROCEDURE

ADJOURN — To end a meeting officially. A motion to adjourn is undebatable.

AGENDA — A list of the order of work to be considered.

AMEND — To change by striking out, inserting, substituting, or adding to a motion being considered.

AYE OR NO — Yes or No in a voiced vote; a member can request a recount by a show of hands.

BALLOT — A written vote, which assures secrecy.

BYLAWS — Set rules of procedure; they are more specific than the constitution.

CHAIR — Short for chairman.

CHAIRMAN — The presiding officer, usually the president of the club.

COMMITTEE OF THE WHOLE — The entire club when it enters into informal discussion of a proposal or intended action.

CONSTITUTION — The basic rules guiding a club.

DECISION OF THE CHAIR — A ruling made by the chairman. It may be appealed by a member; a majority vote settles the dispute.

DIVISION OF ASSEMBLY — A request for a standing or show-of-hands vote, instead of a voiced vote of "Aye" or "No."

FLOOR — The member recognized by the chairman is regarded as having the floor.

GAVEL — The traditional mallet used by the presiding officer to attain order; it is also a symbol of his high office.

INCIDENTAL MOTION — A motion that assists in clarifying a main motion, or helps to speed up the business at hand.

INFORMAL DISCUSSION — Free discussion of a proposal without making a motion.

MAIN MOTION — A proposal for action by the group. It must be discussed and voted on by the members.

Majority Vote — More than one-half the legal votes cast. Blank votes and members not voting are ignored in determining the majority.

Minutes — The record of a meeting. It is usually kept by the secretary, and is reported for approval of the members at the next meeting.

Motion — A proposal for action by the group. It should be introduced by the words, "*I move that. . . .*" It should be affirmative.

New Business — Motions presented for discussion for the first time.

Nomination — A proposal of a candidate for office. The nominee has the right to withdraw his name from contest; a majority vote elects.

Oppose — To work actively against a proposal or candidate.

Order of Business — The same as *agenda*; the order in which items are to be taken up by the group.

Out of Order — A main motion is out of order when there is a main motion already on the floor. An amendment is out of order when it does not apply to the intention of the main motion or when more than two amendments are suggested. A remark or action is out of order when it violates the rights of any member.

Outrank — A motion that has prior claim to discussion outranks another motion: for example, the motion to adjourn the meeting outranks all other motions.

Parliamentary Law — The body of laws and regulations developed for the orderly conduct of a meeting.

Point of Order — A demand addressed to the chairman that a rule be enforced or a mistake be corrected; the chairman rules on the demand.

Precedence — The right of one motion to be considered before another. (*See* Simplified Chart of Motions.)

Previous Question — A motion to stop debate; requires a two-thirds vote; is not debatable, hence requires immediate vote.

Put the Question — A parliamentary phrase meaning to take a vote — used when the chairman wants to take a vote. He asks: *"Shall the question now be put?"*

Question — Proposal for action presented in the form of a motion.

Question of Information — Request by a member for information; the form is, *"I rise to a point of information."*

Question of Privilege — Request for the observance of a member's rights; usually refers to personal comfort, improper remarks, or the presence of non-members at the club meeting.

Quorum — Number of members needed to hold a meeting; the bylaws indicate the percentage required.

Recess — A request for a short break in the meeting; may be called for a definite number of minutes or at the discretion of the chairman.

Reconsider — A motion to review a previous decision.

Refer to a Committee — A motion to delegate a problem to a small group for special study, sometimes with power to make a decision and carry it out.

Report — Recommendations submitted to the group by a committee.

Resolution — A formal proposal submitted to the group; it usually gives reasons, which are prefaced with the word "whereas."

Rising Vote — A form of voting in which members stand and are counted as being for or against a motion.

Second — Endorsement of a motion; done by calling out, *"I second the motion."*

Sergeant at Arms — A person appointed to maintain order during a meeting.

Seriatim — Means of considering a motion section by section or paragraph by paragraph, usually used when constitutions or resolutions are being discussed and amended.

Special Meeting — A meeting called to discuss a single question and no other.

Standing Committee — A committee selected to handle only one aspect of club procedure, such as a membership committee or a treasury committee. Standing committees have the same term of office as the officers, usually one year.

Table — To put a proposal aside for another time.

Take from the Table — To renew a proposal. This requires a majority vote.

Tellers — Members selected by the chairman to collect and count ballots.

Tie Vote — A vote in which each side has an equal number; the deciding vote is cast by the chairman if he has not previously voted.

Unanimous Vote — A vote completely for or against; usually used for a show of confidence, as in an election.

Unfinished Business — A motion being discussed at a meeting, but interrupted by a motion to adjourn; such a motion comes up at the next regular meeting as unfinished business.

SIMPLIFIED CHART OF MOTIONS

Motion	*Purpose*	*Debatable*	*Amendable*	*Priority**	*Vote*
PRIVILEGED MOTIONS: *Require immediate action because they involve personal rights.*					
Adjourn	Close meeting	No	No	(1)	Majority
Recess	Interrupt meeting	No	Yes (as to time)	(2)	Majority
Question of privilege	Assert rights	No	No	(3)	Chair rules
SUBSIDIARY MOTIONS: *Motions used to dispose of or change main motions.*					
Place on the table	To put aside or postpone	No	No	(4)	Majority
Order previous question	Close debate	No	No	(5)	Two-thirds
Postpone to a definite time	Delay action	Yes	Yes (as to time)	(6)	Majority
Refer to committee	Needs more study	Yes	Yes	(7)	Majority
Amend	Change or modify	Yes	Yes	(8)	Majority

Motion	*Purpose*	*Debatable*	*Amendable*	*Priority**	*Vote*
INCIDENTAL MOTIONS: *Motions that arise during debate; are readily settled.*					
Point of order	Assert rights	No	No		Chair rules
Point of information	Request information	No	No		Chair replies
Appeal the decision of the Chair	Assert rights	Yes	No		Majority
Parliamentary inquiry	Request to clarify rules	No	No		Chair replies
Nominate	Elections	Yes	No		Majority
PRINCIPAL MOTIONS: *The final action to be taken; or a change of mind.*					
Main motion	To propose new business	Yes	Yes	(9)	Majority
Special order of business	To speed action	Yes	Yes		Two-thirds
Reconsider	Change a decision	Yes	No		Majority

*PRIORITY (precedence) — The right of one motion to be considered before another.

INDEX